Stencils and Prints

Deri Robins

QED Publishing

Copyright © QED Publishing 2004

First published in the UK in 2004 by
QED Publishing
A Quarto Group Company
226 City Road
London, EC1V 2TT

www.qed-publishing.co.uk

A Catalogue record for this book
is available from the British Library.

ISBN 1 84538 281 1

Written by Deri Robins
Designed by Wladek Szechter/Louise Morley
Edited by Sian Morgan/Matthew Harvey
Artwork by Melanie Grimshaw
Photographer Michael Wicks
With thanks to Victoria

Creative Director: Louise Morley
Editorial Manager: Jean Coppendale

Printed and bound in China

The words in **bold** are
explained in the Glossary
on page 30.

Contents

Print kit

Most printing materials are simple and cheap. Apart from poster paints and brushes, you can find everything you need for printing around the house.

Paper and card

You will need lots of newspaper to protect your work surface. You will also need paper to print onto, ranging from smooth drawing paper to rough **sugar paper**. Scrap paper is always useful for trying out your ideas – ask adults to save any that is being recycled.

Papers with different textures

Poster paints

Card is useful, so keep cardboard tubes and packing material. You can buy special card for **stencilling** from craft shops – although most thin card will do, such as cereal boxes.

Paints and inks

Poster paint is fine for most types of printing. Sometimes you can add a little **PVA glue** or washing-up liquid to stop the paint drying out too fast. Printing inks are excellent, too.

For **marbling**, you will need oil paints – make your own by mixing powder paints into cooking oil. Remember that you need to thin oil paint with **white spirit**, not water.

You'll need to buy special paints from a craft shop for printing on fabric.

Tools and brushes

A **paint roller** is useful, but you can also get good results by applying the paint to your **printers** with a brush. For stencilling, you need a stippling brush with short, stubby bristles. An old toothbrush will be useful for **spattering**.

For some projects, you will need a **craft knife**. Handle it with care. Make sure that your work surface is protected and that an adult is present to help you.

Bits and pieces

One of the most useful parts of your print kit will be your junk box. Almost anything can be used for printing! Keep scraps of bubble wrap, fabric, card, old ice-lolly sticks, buttons, sponge, string, broken toys and old tools – there are more suggestions throughout the book.

Ink

Stippling brush

Watercolour paints

Sponge roller

TIP

Keep scraps of coloured fabric, coloured paper and sweet wrappers, and paste them into a **scrapbook** or **sketchbook**. See how many shades of one colour you can find.

Print effects

Any pattern made by pressing something down on a surface is printing. You've probably done it by accident! You can make beautiful shapes and **textures** from ordinary things, and make repeat patterns quickly. Let your imagination go wild!

Basic printing

You have ready-made printing equipment at the end of your fingers! Dip your fingers, thumbs and the side of your hands into thick paint and press them down on paper.

What designs can you make? Use your feet or put on a thick layer of lipstick and press firmly on a piece of paper for luscious lip prints.

Found printers

There are plenty of objects that make wonderful patterns, such as doilies, lace, the ends of straws, tools, keys and fruit and vegetables.

Broccoli prints

Wheat prints

Feather print

What else can you think of?

Extra ideas

You could frame your prints, or even wear them! Try making cheap wrapping paper and gift tags that are better than the versions in the shops!

Prints can even be used to decorate old furniture, walls and fabric (but always ask an adult first).

TIPS

Try printing on different types of paper: brown paper, newspaper and tissue all work well. Try using **PVA glue** instead of paint – sprinkle glitter over while it's wet.

Mirror printing

This is one of the simplest and quickest ways to print. The method is always the same, but every print is different.

Easy butterfly blob print

WHAT YOU NEED:
- Thick poster paints
- Paper
- A brush

1 Fold the paper in half. Open it out and paint some thick blobs on one side, roughly in the shape of half a butterfly. Make sure the paint goes right into the fold, but not over it.

TIP
This works well for **symmetrical** shapes, such as flowers or leaves. See how many you can come up with.

1

2

2 Fold the paper over. Press down firmly, and then open it up.

TIP
Experiment with string of different thicknesses and texture.

2 Fold a piece of paper in half, then open it back out, as you did for the mirror print. Lay the strings carefully on one side of the paper, with one end of each string sticking out over the edge.

3 Fold the other half of the paper over again and press your hand firmly over the surface. Keeping your hand pressed down, pull out the strings by their ends. Open the paper to see your swirly string picture!

String prints

String prints make fascinating, swirly patterns.

WHAT YOU NEED:
- Paper • Poster paints
- Saucers • String
- Scissors

1 Cut three lengths of string. Put three different-coloured poster paints into separate saucers. Put a piece of string in each saucer. Make sure they are well coated with paint.

Printing from card

One of the most common methods of printing is to use blocks. These can be complicated or very simple. You can make your own blocks for printing – the easiest are simple shapes cut out of card.

Print kit

Save as many different types of card as possible – **corrugated** card is great for stripy, textured prints. You can use all parts of the card – the smooth sides are good for printing blocks of colour, while the edges are useful for lines and curves. Use the ends of straws or cardboard tubes to make circles or ovals.

TIP

To make your blocks easier to use, glue a small piece of cork or **polystyrene** to the back to serve as a handle.

Print a greetings card

Try making blocks for a simple greetings card. You can re-use them to make a batch of cards – perfect for Christmas.

WHAT YOU NEED:

- Thick poster paints
- Card and paper • A brush

1 Sketch out your ideas for the card design on scrap paper. Keep the shapes simple.

2 Now cut out the shapes you need for your design. You can glue small pieces of **polystyrene** to the back to serve as handles.

3 Brush the largest printing block with paint. Then press it firmly onto the paper and peel it off to reveal the print beneath.

4 When the first colour is dry, do the same with the smaller blocks until your picture is finished. Try not to smudge!

5 You can add details by printing with the top of pen lids.

TIP
Remember when you make a print that the finished print will be a mirror image of your printing block!

Making blocks

By gluing various objects to small bits of wood, you can make printing blocks that you can re-use over and over again. See what you can find around the house.

Simple kit

Glue bits of string to small pieces of wood or thick card in an interesting shape for simple prints.

Try shapes from foam, rubber, sponge, old keys, paper clips, dried pasta, buttons, buckles, old toys or broken jewellery. Just about anything will do!

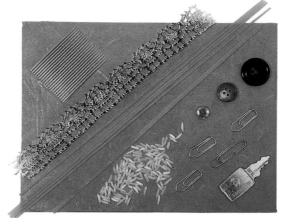

Let your imagination run wild – but don't forget to ask permission first.

You can paint on lots of bright colours to get a rainbow effect.

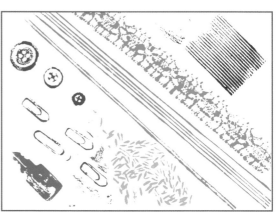

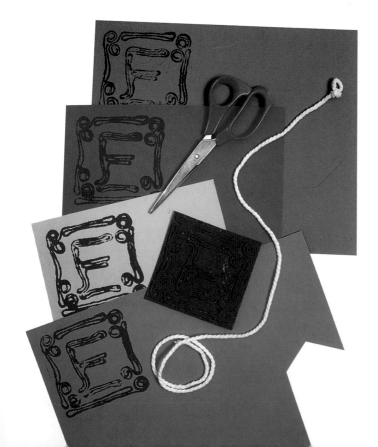

Make a bookplate

Glue string onto one face of a block of wood to form the shape of your initial (remember to do it back to front). Add a few swirls and decorations, and use it to print your initial in the front page of your books. Or you could use it to make headed notepaper.

Sponge stamps

These are ideal for crisp, clean prints. They are expensive to buy – but you can make your own.

WHAT YOU NEED:
- A sponge
- A craft knife
- A brush
- Thick paint
- Paper

3 Brush or roll paint over the raised surface and then press the stamp down onto the paper.

Sponges are also great for smaller patterns, such as wallpaper for a dolls' house. You could even print your own 'postage stamps'.

Try printing a trail of animal tracks. Glue thin stamps around the outside of a stiff cardboard tube, and use it as a roller printer.

1 Draw a simple design on the soft side of the sponge.

2 Ask an adult to cut away the parts around the design using a craft knife.

Prints from nature

Some of the most delicate prints are made from objects from the natural world. Feathers, leaves, flowers and wood all make intricate prints. Using **printers**, you can make a pattern that would take hours to paint with a brush.

Print kit

See what ready-made printers you can find when you are out on a walk. Some, such as feathers and bits of bark, will keep more or less forever, while green leaves will have to be used before they dry out.

Roll or brush thick paint carefully over leaves, ferns, corn stalks etc. and press them down on paper to make a print. Experiment with different effects and colours. For example, a white leaf or fern print looks great on dark paper.

TIP

Leaves don't last very long, but you can make long-lasting leaf-shaped printers! Just trace around the leaves onto thick card, cut them out and use them as printing blocks.

You can use feathers to create a bird-bath picture like this.

Leaf prints

Choose three different types of leaf and brush each one with different coloured paint to print a pattern.

WHAT YOU NEED:

- A collection of leaves – at least three different types.
- Bright, thick poster paint
- Paper • A brush

1 Brush a bright colour over one of the leaves, and press it down onto dark coloured paper. Do this several times, then leave it to dry.

2 Take a different leaf, and use a different coloured paint. Print onto the paper, overlapping the first leaf prints.

3 Carry on printing until hardly any of the dark background shows through.

Try printing while the first colour is still wet. Use **pastel** colours on white paper for an airy and delicate effect.

Brush paint onto the back of the leaf and press it onto the paper.

1

2

3

Mount up your picture on coloured paper and place it on your wall.

Potato prints

A potato print is a cross between a food **printer** and a printing block.

Print kit

All you need to make a potato printer is a big potato and a **craft knife**. Your printer won't last very long, but if you slice off the old design, you can start again on the fresh surface. Other root vegetables make good printing blocks, too – try a few of them and see which ones work best.

WHAT YOU NEED:
- A large potato
- A sharp pencil
- A craft knife
- Thick paints
- Paper

1 Ask an adult to cut the potato in half. Draw a simple design in the cut surface with a sharp pencil. Try a butterfly, a flower or a star.

2 Ask the adult to cut around the design, and remove the excess from around the edges so that your design sticks out. Brush paint over the surface of the design.

TAKE CARE !

3 Press the painted surface firmly onto paper. Rock the printer gently, so that all parts of the design touch the paper.

Try coloured paper and contrasting paints for colourful wrapping paper.

TIP

It's fun to make your own gift tags. Cut lots of small rectangles from thin coloured card or stiff paper, and fold them in half. Punch a hole in the top-left corner to thread some ribbon through. Then just use potato printers to make a design. You could make an interesting border around the edges, too.

TIP

Use a **pastry cutter** to make an instant printer! Just press the cutter into a potato, and ask an adult to cut away around the outside before removing the cutter.

Your friends and family will much prefer a hand-made gift tag with your own design on it.

TIP

Try using different coloured paints on different parts of a butterfly to get some really interesting, multi-coloured results!

Prints from food

It's amazing how many ready-made **printers** you can find in the kitchen. Biscuits often have patterns, pasta comes in all sorts of unusual shapes and fruit and vegetables can be cut into halves, rounds and quarters. All of them make great prints.

Print kit

Try using tangerine segments, peppers cut in half, carrots cut into rounds or sliced down the middle, the leaves from a cabbage … the possibilities are endless. You will get quite different results by cutting an apple length ways – and then across the middle.

Foody wallpaper

Once you have experimented with different food prints, you could make a wallpaper design. Draw light **guidelines** first with a ruler and pencil, and then build up a design with one, two or three shapes.

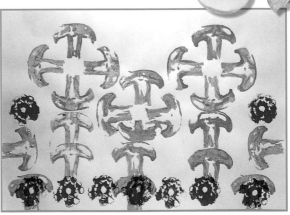

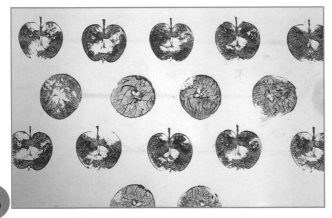

You can use vegetables and fruit to make patterns or abstract images.

Market stall

This is an impressive project you can make from things you've probably got around the house. Be sure to ask an adult before you raid the fridge for foods to use for printing!

WHAT YOU NEED:
- A cardboard box
- Fruits and vegetables
- Scissors
- A craft knife
- Thick paints
- Paper • Glue

1 Ask an adult to cut the side flaps off the box: the bottom flap makes the base, and the top flap supports the **awning**. Add **pillars** made by rolling up tubes of the card and taping them together. Glue these inside the outer edges of the box. Paint the inside of the box.

2 Ask the adult to cut the awning from card. Paint it brightly. You could give your shop a name too, and paint it on. Glue the awning to the front of the box and pillars.

3 Make lots of fruit and vegetable prints and cut them out. You'll need something to support them. Use smaller boxes or ask an adult to cut box shapes from white card. Glue the boxes and prints to the front of the stall. The grapes can be hung from string.

Make an appetizing assortment of fruit and veg prints.

Make a Pop Art print

The American Pop Artist **Andy Warhol** often repeated the same image several times over to make bold, bright paintings and prints. Here's how to make a really striking Pop Art print for your wall.

WHAT YOU NEED:

- A ruler and pencil
- Bright paints
- Bubble wrap
- Black felt tip
- A simple printer – this could be a card or wooden block, a potato or a piece of fruit
- Thick paper or thin card
- Brushes
- **PVA glue**

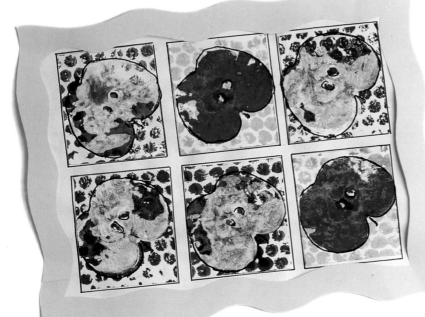

1 Brush brightly coloured paint over the bubble wrap, and press down onto the paper to print a dotty pattern. Do this several times, and use a different colour for each piece of paper. Use the ruler and pencil to divide the prints into neat squares, each the same size.

2 Glue the squares to a piece of card to make a **chequered** effect. Leave a wide border. Brush paint over your **printer** and press it onto the first square – choose a colour that **contrasts** with the dots. Red and green, blue and orange and yellow and purple make good contrasts.

3 Carry on printing onto the squares until every one is filled. Use the black felt tip to go over the lines of each of the squares. Cut some card to make a frame. Paint it in a bright colour and then cut a wavy outline with scissors. Tape a loop of thread to the back so that you can hang it up.

The dots in your picture will make it look like the prints that Andy Warhol made.

Make a Pop Art notebook

Protect the print with sticky-backed plastic. Lay an open notebook on the back of the print, and draw around it. Draw a border of 6cm. Cut flaps in the border, and fold them over the covers of the book, gluing them in place. Glue the first and last pages of the notebook to the covers, to hide the flaps.

Marbling

Marbling works because oil and water don't mix – the oil in the paint stays on the surface of the water, and will stick to the paper when you make a print. The swirling oil makes wonderful patterns.

Marbling paper

Marbling paper needs to be thick enough not to turn soggy in the water, but thin enough for you to be able to peel it off the surface.

WHAT YOU NEED:
- Oil paints (you could use powder paints mixed with cooking oil)
- **White spirit** • Brushes
- An old baking tin or tray
- Newspaper • Paper

1 Mix your paint with white spirit until it is runny enough to fall off the brush in blobs. Half-fill the tin with water, then flick or pour the paint onto the surface. Try using two colours to begin with. Swirl the surface gently with the end of your brush.

2 Lay a sheet of paper very gently on top of the water, smoothing away any air bubbles. Take care not to push the paper under the surface.

3 Lift the paper gently from one end, and leave it to dry.

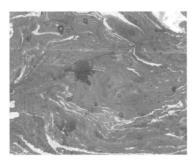

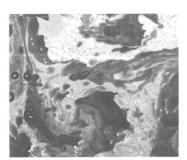

Marble collage

Marbled paper can be used to make great collages, with interesting patterns in the paint. Draw and colour in a simple shape, such as a bird or animal. Cut up the picture, so that each area of colour makes a separate shape.

Use these shapes as **templates** to cut identical shapes from your marbled paper. Then just stick the marbled shapes together in the right order.

TIP

Try adding a little wallpaper paste to the water – this helps you to swirl the paint into a feathery pattern. It's particularly good for watery effects, such as in this pond.

Monoprints

A monoprint is made by pressing a piece of paper over a painted design, and lifting it off. The **textures** and shapes you get would be impossible to create by painting – they may not always be successful, but when they are, they can be brilliant!

TIP

When you roll your paint out onto the flat surface, you could mix two colours together to create an interesting graduation between one colour and the next. You could also try experimenting with multi-coloured monoprints, using lots of different colours.

Print kit

You will need a really smooth surface to print from – a piece of formica, a mirror or a shiny baking tray are ideal. Water-based printing inks give the best results, but you can also use thick paint. Mix the paint with a little **PVA glue** or washing-up liquid to keep it from drying out too quickly. Just as with the mirror prints on page 8, a monoprint (meaning 'one print') can never be repeated.

TAKE CARE !

Be careful if you are using a glass top to print on – you will need adult help. Check with an adult before you use a table or other piece of furniture to make your monoprint.

Drawing a monoprint

In this project, you draw a shape to create a monoprint beneath.

1 Roll bands of colour onto the smooth surface, and lay the paper lightly on top.

2 Using a pencil, crayon or knitting needle, draw a design on the paper – try to press the paper just on the lines you are drawing.

3 Lift up the paper gently, making sure not smudge the image. Leave it to dry out completely.

Stencils

Stencilling was very popular among the early settlers in North America, who could not buy wallpaper or decorated furniture. Practise stencilling on paper or card first – when you feel confident enough, you could use your stencils to decorate your room.

Print kit

There are plenty of ready-made stencils to print from. You can also buy stencils from craft shops. You will need a brush with short, stubby bristles to make stencils. The paint should be almost dry, and you should dab it over the stencil. This technique is called 'stippling'.

Make your own stencils

You can use your stencils to decorate a whole range of things. Ask an adult for help with cutting.

WHAT YOU NEED:
- Stencilling card (any thin card will do) • Tape
- A short-haired brush
- Thick paint • A pencil
- A **craft knife**
- Paper

TAKE CARE !

1 Draw a simple design onto the card with a pencil.

2 Ask an adult to cut out the shape with a craft knife.

3 Tape the stencil to the sheet of paper. Using an almost dry brush, stipple the paint over the hole in the stencil, making sure that you go right up to the edges.

Stencil spatter

Instead of stippling your stencil design, you can spatter! Just load the paint onto an old toothbrush, point the brush at the paper and run a stiff piece of card over the bristles. Use interesting shapes such as leaves, keys or tools. What happens if you move them slightly, and then spatter again with another colour?

TIP

Use a simple stencilled design to decorate writing paper and matching envelopes. Or stencil wrapping paper – try using spray paint for really fast results.

Spray stencilling

For really quick stencilling, you could use spray paint. Spray paints come in lots of interesting colours, such as silver – as used below.

1 Make a large stencil with a repeat pattern. Lay it over coloured paper and spray paint over it.

Instead of cutting holes, you can cut shapes, lay them on the paper and then spray them to get a negative image beneath.

2 Make sure you cover each part of the stencil, and then lift the stencil off. Leave it a few minutes to dry.

Printing pictures

The more you experiment with different kinds of **printers**, the more ideas you are likely to get for your pictures. You can mix prints with collage and paint effects, too. Try to think about your prints in a new way – a cabbage leaf print may look just like a cabbage leaf – but it would also make a great tree!

Trees in the park

In this project, you can use cabbage leaves to create intricate tree shapes that would take a long time to draw or paint.

WHAT YOU NEED:
- Cabbage leaves
- Thick paints
- Thin, watered-down paints
- Brushes • Paper
- Card • Scissors
- Glue

A stippling brush (one with short, stiff bristles) is good for brushing paint onto the cabbage leaf.

1 Paint the background very quickly, using a wide, soft brush and thin, watered-down paints. Leave it to dry (if you tape it down to your work surface, it stops the paper wrinkling).

2 Now make lots of tree prints, using cabbage leaves of different sizes. Use a good variety of colours, from yellow-green to greens with a brown or bluish shade.

3 When the trees are dry, cut them out carefully and glue them to the picture. Finish the picture by printing the fence, using the edge of a piece of card brushed with brown paint.

Can you make a print collage like this of your favourite view? Or how about a fantasy landscape – such as a spaceship landing on a distant planet?

TIP

Cauliflower and broccoli florets make good trees, too. Simple shapes torn from paper make delicate clouds, misty mountains, icebergs or rough rocks. Sandpaper is perfect for cliffs.

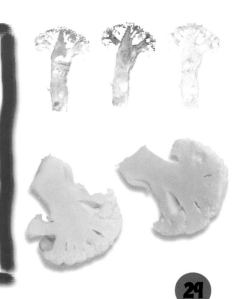

Glossary

Andy Warhol   American artist famous for his colourful prints (1928–1987)

awning   the cover at the front of a shop that keeps the sun and rain off

chequered   a pattern made up of squares of different colours

contrasts   when two colours stand out when placed next to each other

corrugated   card that has a series of ridges in it

craft knife   a sharp knife; you need adult help to use one

guidelines   lines on a piece of paper to help you place your images

paint roller   a tool for covering large areas evenly with paint

pastel   soft, delicate colours

pastry cutter   a tool for cutting shapes out of pastry

pillars   strong supports for buildings

polystyrene   an artificial, lightweight material that can be cut into shapes

printers   objects to which paint is applied to make a print

PVA glue   a white glue that can be mixed with water and which dries clear

scrapbook   a collection of materials for printing, kept in a book

sketchbook   a book for making quick drawings and designs

spattering   to spray a picture with paint with a brush

sugar paper   thick, textured paper

symmetrical   a shape that is the same on both sides

templates   shapes cut out out to help you copy the shapes many times

textures   the surfaces of things, for example, rough or smooth

Index

Notes to teachers

The projects in this book are aimed at Key Stage 2 children. You can use them as stand-alone lessons, or as a part of other subjects. The ideas in the book offer children inspiration, but you should always encourage them to draw from their own imagination and first-hand observation as well as from memory and their own experience.

Sourcing ideas

All art projects should tap into children's interests and be relevant to their lives and experiences. Some stimulating starting points might be: found objects, discussions about their family and pets, hobbies, TV programmes or topical events.

Encourage children to source their own ideas and references, from books, magazines, the Internet or CD-ROMs.

Digital cameras can create reference material (pictures of landscapes, people or animals) and also be used alongside children's finished work (see below).

Other lessons can be an ideal springboard for an art project – for example, a seasonal festival could be the start of a card-printing project, or a science lesson could lead to printing from seed heads or cross sections of fruit.

Use recycling as a basis for print activities. Ask the children to come up with new uses for broken toys and other objects.

Encourage children to keep a sketchbook of their ideas, and to collect other images and objects to help them develop their drawings.

Give pupils as many first-hand experiences as possible through visits and contact with creative people.

Evaluating work

It's important and motivating for children to share their work with others, and to compare ideas and methods. Encourage them to talk about their work. What do they like best about it? How would they do it differently next time?

Show the children examples of other artists' work – how did they tackle the same subject? Do the children like the work? Why? Why not?

Help children to judge the originality and value of their work, to appreciate the different qualities in others' work and to value ways of working that are different from their own. Display all the children's work.

Going further

Look at ways to develop projects. Many of the ideas in this book could be adapted into painting, collage and print-making. Remember to use image-enhancing computer software and digital scanners to enhance, build up and juxtapose images.

Show the children how to set up a class art gallery on the school website. Having their work displayed professionally makes them feel that their work is valued.